OXFORD First Book of *Science*

OXFORD

First Book of Science

Nina Morgan

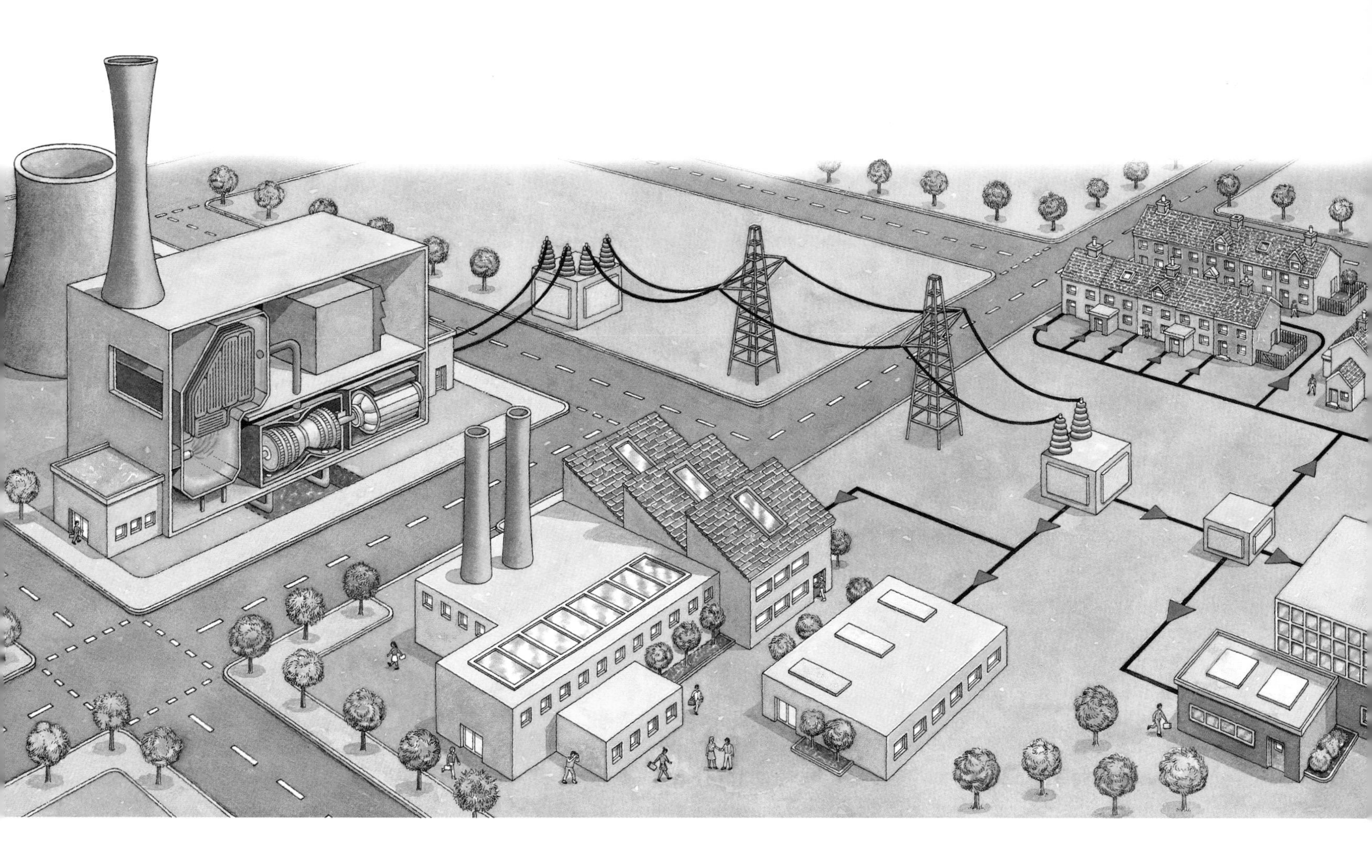

OXFORD
UNIVERSITY PRESS

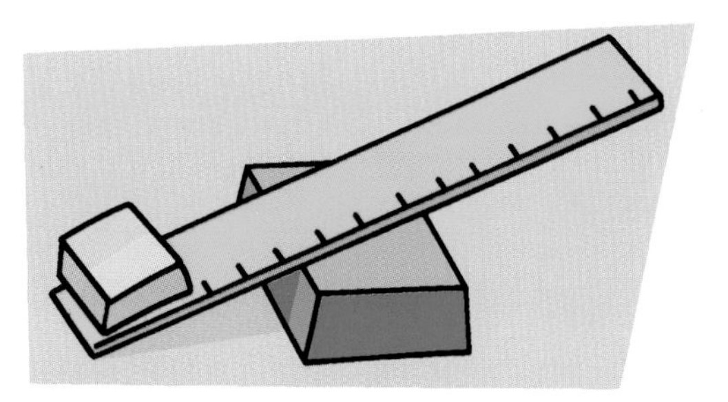

OXFORD
UNIVERSITY PRESS

Great Clarendon Street, Oxford OX2 6DP

Oxford University Press is a department of the University of Oxford.
It furthers the University's objective of excellence in research, scholarship,
and education by publishing worldwide in

Oxford New York

Auckland Bangkok Buenos Aires Cape Town Chennai
Dar es Salaam Delhi Hong Kong Istanbul Karachi Kolkata
Kuala Lumpur Madrid Melbourne Mexico City Mumbai Nairobi
São Paulo Shanghai Taipei Tokyo Toronto

Oxford is a registered trade mark of Oxford University Press
in the UK and in certain other countries

First published in hardback 1999
First published in paperback 2000
This edition 2003

British Library Cataloguing in Publication Data available

ISBN 0-19-910984-2 Paperback

5 7 9 10 8 6

Printed in China

Contents

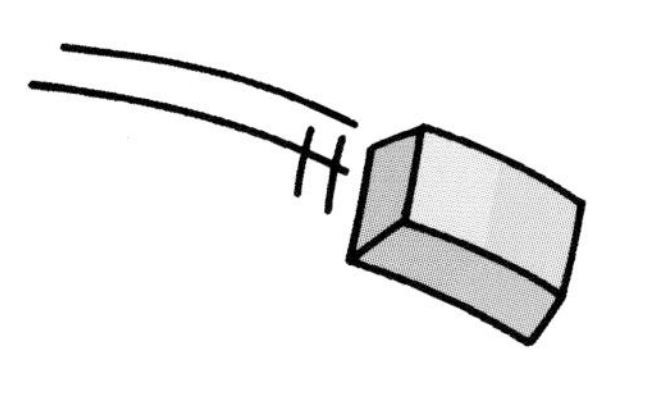

What is Science?

Have you ever wondered how plants get their food, or why it is light during the day, but dark at night? Science can help you find the answers! Science helps us to find out all about the world we live in and how it works.

▶ If you want to know how tall something is, you can measure it using a metre stick or a tape measure.

Careful looking

How do scientists work? They ask a lot of questions and find ways to answer them. To do this, they look at things carefully and write down what they see. Sometimes they carry out special tests, called experiments, and carefully measure what happens. You can find things out by looking and measuring, too.

▼ If you want to know how fast you can run, you can time yourself using a watch.

▶ If you want to know how heavy something is, you can weigh it using scales.

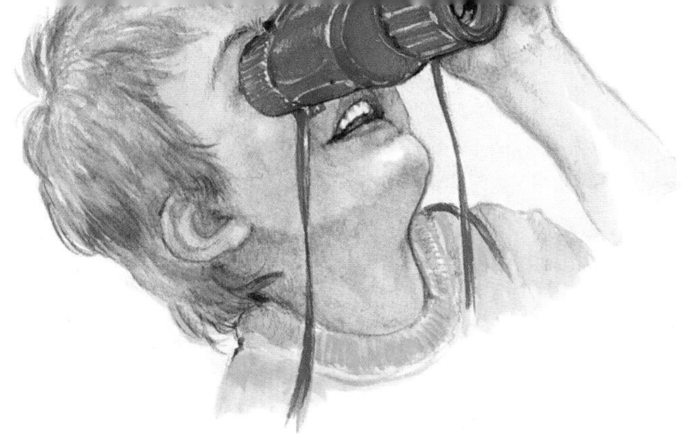

If you want to find out about space, you can look at the stars through binoculars or a telescope.

Using science

Scientists have found out many things. You use these discoveries every day. Each time you switch on a light, ride in a car, ride your bike, watch television or even look at your watch, you are using science.

Try this: Which is biggest?

It is not always easy to tell which glass will hold the most water, especially if the glasses are different shapes. But you can find out with this experiment. It is probably best to do it at the sink.

You will need: *three glasses of different shapes, some water.*

1. Fill one of the glasses to the top with water. Now pour the water carefully into another glass.

2. Does all the water fit? If not, the first glass is bigger. If all the water fits and there is room for more, the second glass is bigger.

3. Fill up the bigger of the two glasses with water again. Now pour the water into the third glass. Does it hold more water, or less?

4. Which glass held the most water? Now that you know which glass is biggest, you can ask for it whenever you have your favourite drink!

All Kinds of Science

There are many different kinds of science. The scientists who study them all want to find out more about the world we live in. And they all use the same ways of doing it – careful looking, measuring, and asking questions.

Which type of scientist should you ask? That depends on your question!

If you want to know how kites fly – ask a physicist. Physics is the study of movement and energy, heat, light and sound.

If you want to know about shapes – ask a mathematician! Mathematicians think about numbers and shapes and the patterns they make.

If you want to know about rocks – ask a geologist! Geologists can tell us what the Earth was like millions of years ago, by looking at the rocks on land and under the sea. They study earthquakes and volcanoes too.

If you want to know about animals or plants – ask a biologist! Biologists study how living things live and grow. They also try to work out how all the different living things are related.

Try this: a scientific study of leaves

Try being a botanist, with this study of leaves.

You will need: *a notebook and pencil, glue*

1. Collect leaves from three different types of tree.

2. Stick one leaf from each tree on a page in your notebook. Write down where you found the leaf and what kind of tree it came from.

3. Make a drawing of the leaf. Label the stem and the veins, and measure how long and how wide it is. Write down how the leaves differ from each other.

If you keep collecting different leaves and putting them in your notebook, you will soon learn a lot about leaves.

▲ If you want to know about the stars – ask an astronomer! Astronomers use telescopes and photographs taken from space to study the stars and planets.

▼ If you want to know what your drink is made of – ask a chemist! Chemists carry out tests to find out what things are made of.

Being Alive

It is easy to see that cats and fish and birds and ants and people are all alive. And everyone knows that stones are not alive. But what about cars? Are they alive? Or trees? Or mushrooms? It is not always so easy to tell if something is alive. You have to look carefully, and ask the right questions.

▼ Scientists ask questions to help them find out whether something is alive or not. For any living thing, the answer to all these questions is "yes".

Does it eat?

Does it move? All living things move, although some move so slowly that it's hard to tell.

Does it breathe? All living things, even if they live in water, have to breathe.

Does it get rid of waste material?

Does it notice when things around it change, and do something?

Does it reproduce itself?

Plants alive

Plants get food, breathe and move, but in different ways from animals. Instead of eating to get food, plants make food in their leaves. They take in air through tiny holes in their leaves, and get rid of waste products the same way. Plants move as they turn to face the Sun and as they grow. They reproduce themselves by producing seeds, or by growing new plants from parts of old ones.

People alive

People may look very different on the outside. But inside, our bodies all have the same parts, and they work in the same way to keep us breathing, eating, moving and playing!

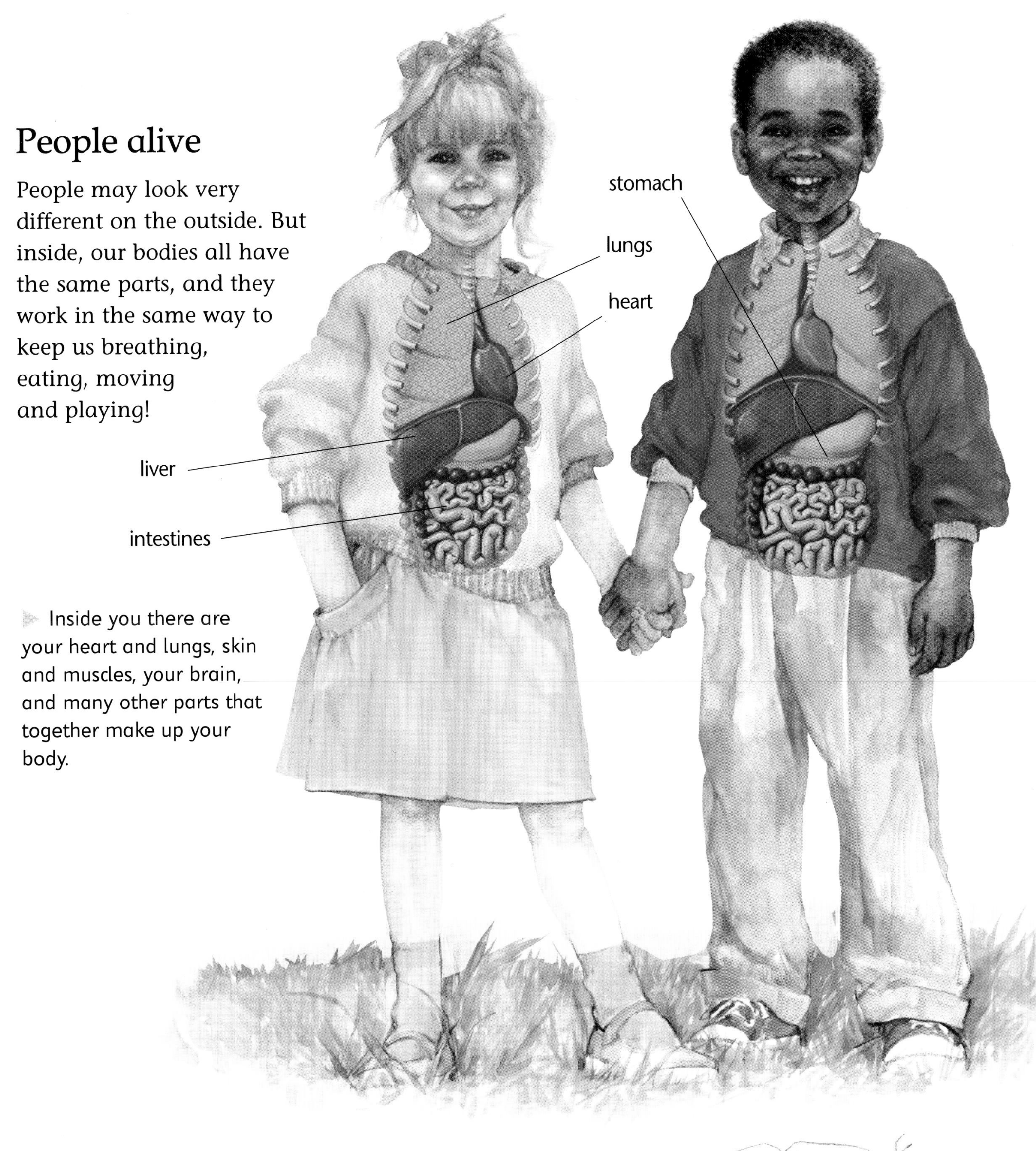

Inside you there are your heart and lungs, skin and muscles, your brain, and many other parts that together make up your body.

Your body is made up of millions of tiny parts, called "cells". Some cells form your brain. Others form your muscles, your bones or your blood. Cells make up every part of you.

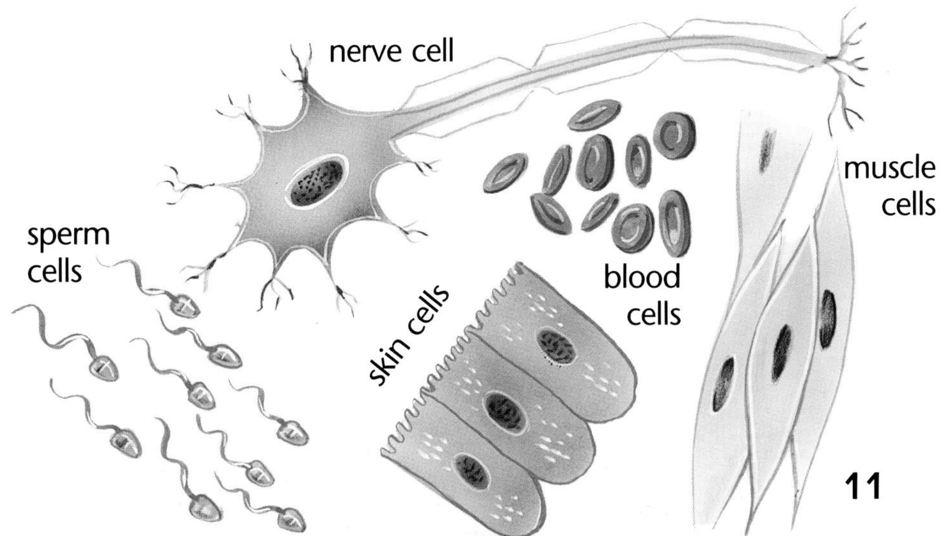

Your Body

Inside your body, many things are happening at the same time. You are breathing, your heart is pumping, your stomach is digesting food, your eyes and brain are reading this book. The parts of your body work together in teams, called "systems". Together, the different systems keep you alive and healthy.

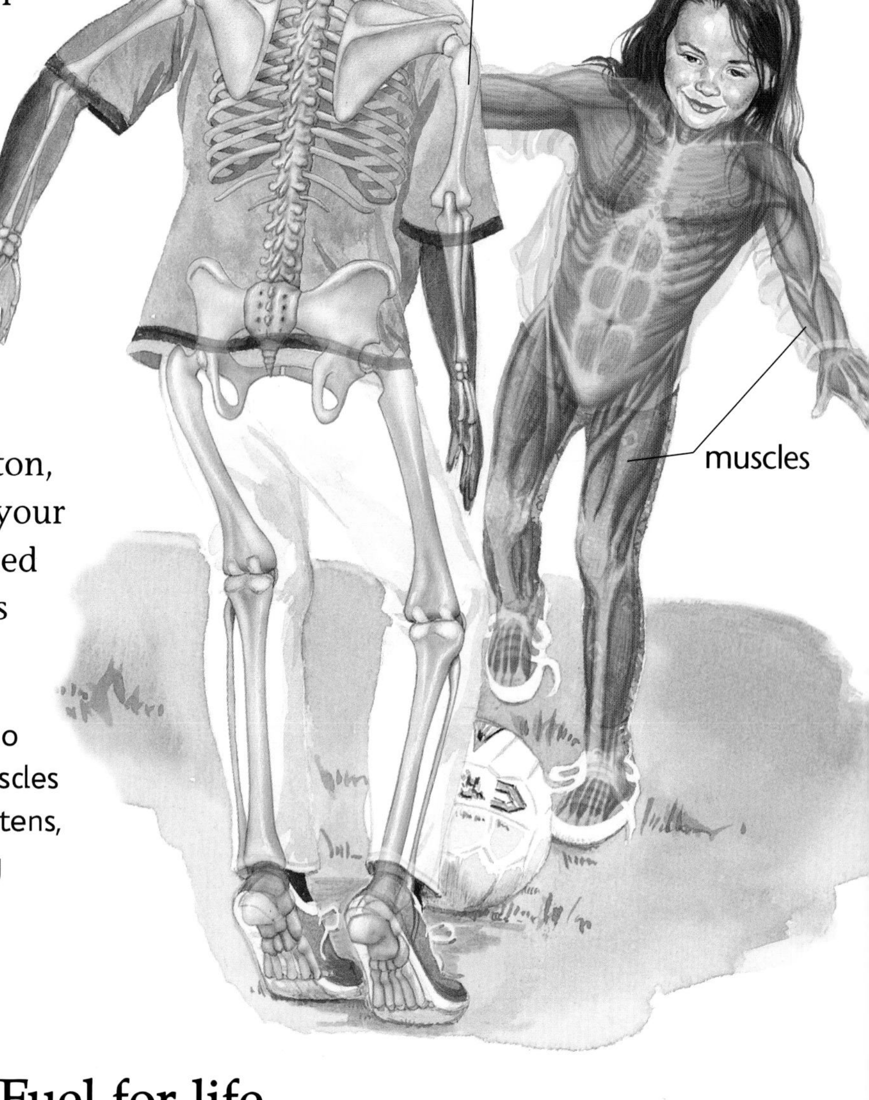

Moving about

You have over 200 bones in your body, and more than 600 muscles. The bones make up your skeleton, which supports your body and protects your insides. Most of your muscles are attached to your skeleton. The bones and muscles work together to move you about.

▶ Your bones are linked together by joints, so that you can bend and move about. Your muscles are fastened to your bones. As a muscle shortens, it pulls on the bones it is fastened to, making them move.

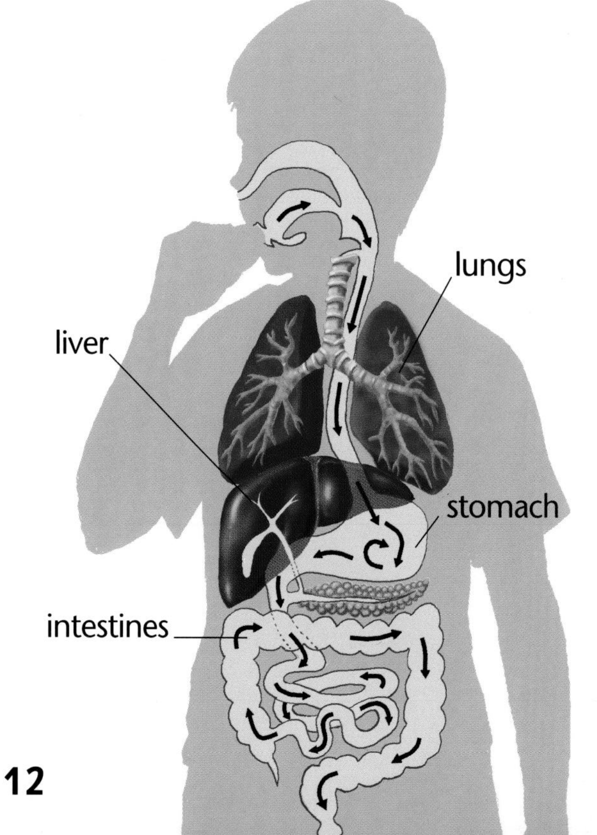

Fuel for life

Your body needs energy to keep it going. Food is the fuel that gives your body the energy it needs, so that you can work, play and think. The air that you breathe in helps your body to break down food and make energy.

◀ Your digestive system breaks down the food you eat, to provide the energy your body needs. It also gets rid of waste. Once food has been broken down, it goes into the blood. Air goes first into your lungs, and then into your blood.

All round the body

Your blood travels all round your body, carrying food and fresh air to every part of you. Your body cells can use the food and air to make energy. Your nerves go to every part of you, too. They carry messages to and from your brain, which is the control centre of your body.

▼ Your blood moves around the body in tiny tubes called "blood vessels". Your heart is the pump that keeps the blood moving.

You use your nose to smell.

You use your eyes to see.

You use your tongue to taste.

You use your ears to hear.

▲ You use your five senses to find out about the world around you.

You use your skin to feel things when you touch them.

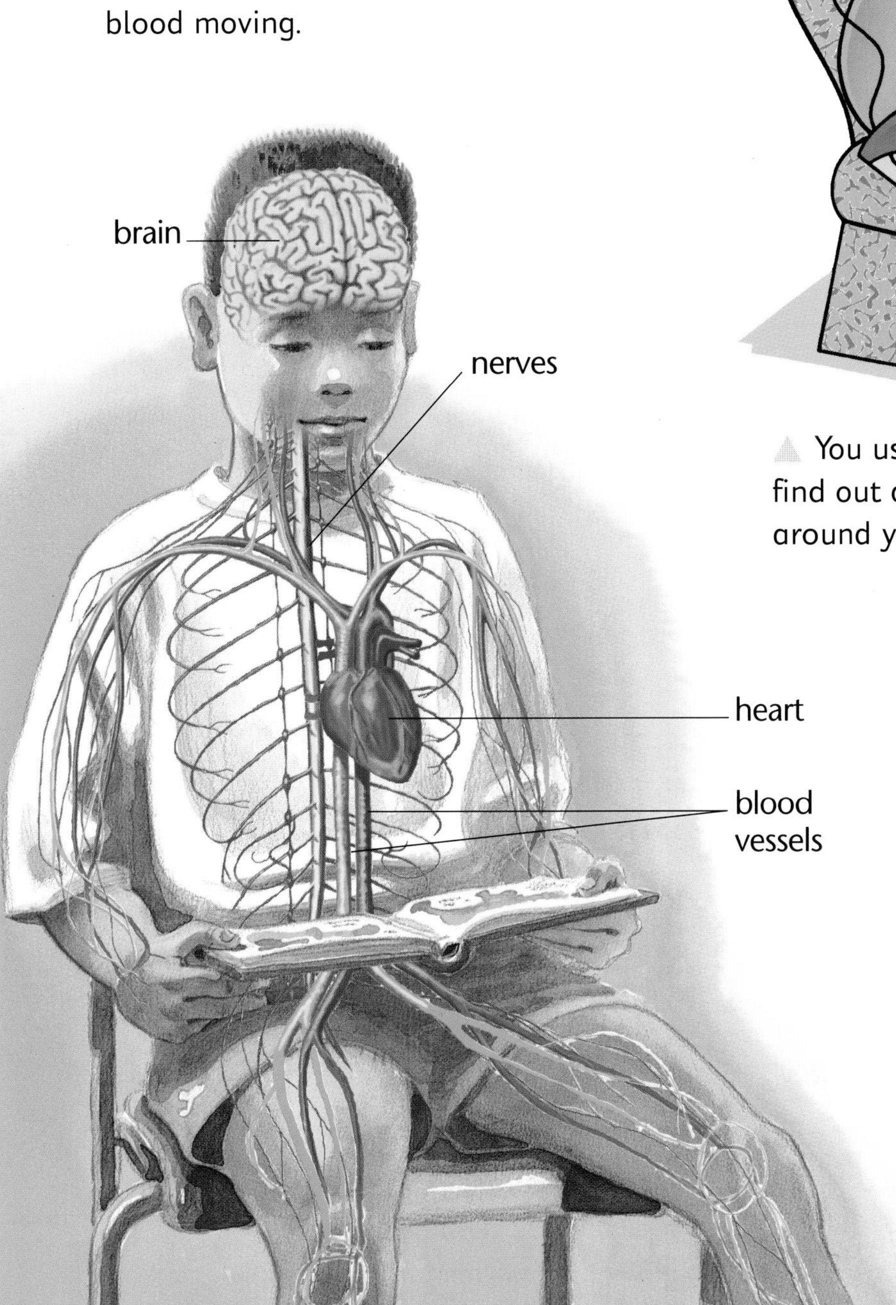

◀ Some nerves carry messages to the brain from your senses, telling you what is happening around you. Other nerves carry messages from your brain to your muscles, telling you how to move.

Growing and Changing

How you've changed! You look very different today from when you were born. And your body will keep on changing as you grow into an adult. Once you are fully grown, your body will change in other ways. All through your life your body will continue to change.

You grew into a person inside a part of your mother's body called the womb. After nine months, you were born!

At first your parents had to do almost everything for you. You could not sit up, or even smile. But you soon learned to do these things.

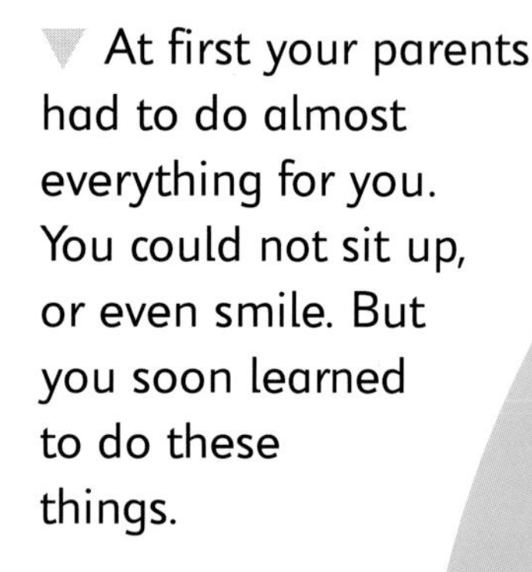

As you got older you learned to control your body better. Now you can do lots of things, like running and jumping, reading and writing, singing and painting. The shape of your body has changed too. You are taller and your legs are longer.

When you are 11 or 12 your body will change shape in a different way. Girls will grow breasts and boys' shoulders will grow wider. These are just some of the many changes taking place in your body to make it possible for you to have children of your own one day.

By the time you are 20 you will probably stop growing taller – but you may still grow fatter!

Use it or lose it!

It is important to look after your body to keep it working well. Otherwise you may become ill. To keep your body healthy, you need to use it. Exercise is important! You should also make sure that you eat the right foods, get enough sleep, and keep yourself clean.

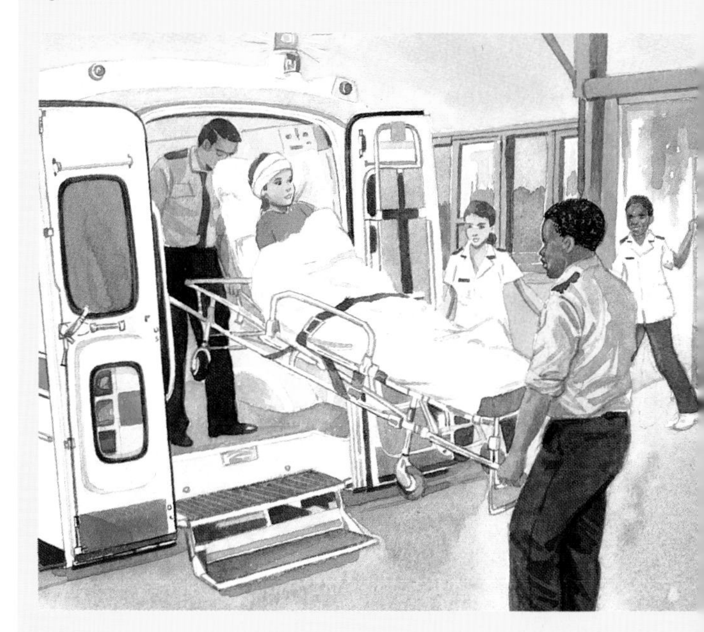

If you become ill or are injured, your body can often heal itself without any help. But if you are very sick, you may need to go to hospital, where doctors and nurses can help you to get well again.

What Are Things Made Of?

Take a look at your house – you will see that it is made of lots of different materials. The walls may be made of bricks. The roof may be made of tiles. The windows are made of glass. Everything inside your house is made of materials too. In fact, everything in the world, even the Earth itself, is made of materials. People use materials to make all sorts of things, from skyscrapers to matches. It is important to choose the right material for the job.

▼ All materials are made of very tiny particles called "atoms". Atoms are too tiny to see. There are lots of different kinds, and they can join together in many ways. In this picture, three atoms are joined together to make a tiny particle of water.

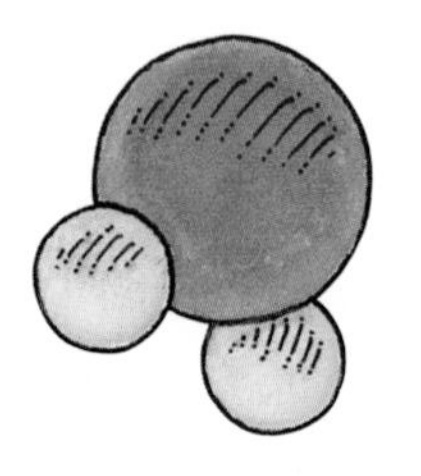

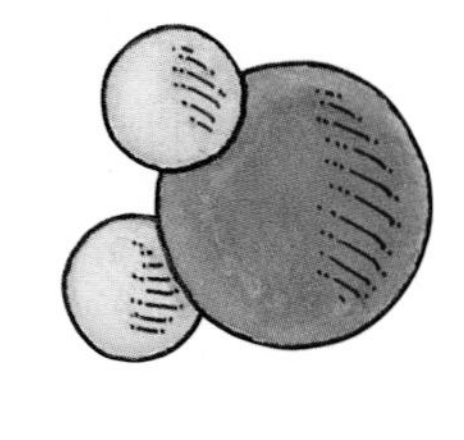

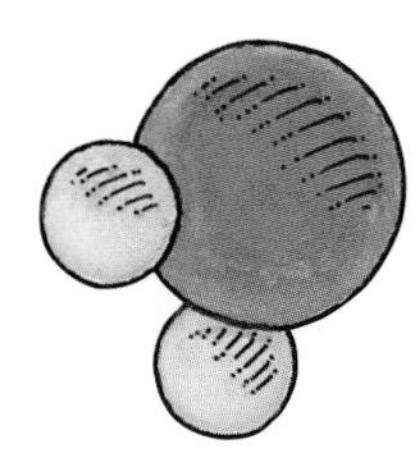

In the bathroom

Look in your bathroom. There are many kinds of material here. Bathtubs, taps, towels, toothbrushes and toilet paper are all made of different materials. Each material was chosen because it has special qualities that make it right for the job it has to do.

Glass is a transparent material. It lets light through. Your bathroom window is made of glass. You can see through it to the outside – if it isn't steamed up!

Bathroom tiles are made of strong, waterproof material called ceramics.

Toilet paper is soft and absorbent. It is flexible, and does not tear even when it is wet.

Cloth is a soft material that bends easily. Clothes are made of cloth. Towels and flannels are made of cloth that soaks up water easily, but does not fall apart.

Plastics

Plastics are amazing materials. Many different types of plastic can be made. They can be clear like glass or hard like wood. They can be soft like cloth or waterproof like ceramics. Plastics are used to make many different things. Cups, bowls, bags, bottles and boxes can all be made of plastics.

▼ Several kinds of plastics are used to make your toothbrush and toothpaste tube. The toothbrush handle and toothpaste tube cap are made of hard, strong plastics. The brush fibres and the toothpaste tube are made of soft plastics that bend easily.

Solids, Liquids and Gases

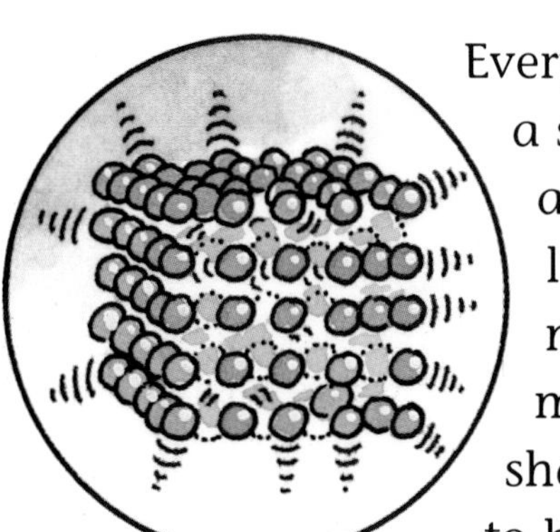

Everything around us is either a solid, a liquid or a gas. The atoms in solids are closely linked together, and do not move around very much. This means solids can keep their shape without any container to hold them.

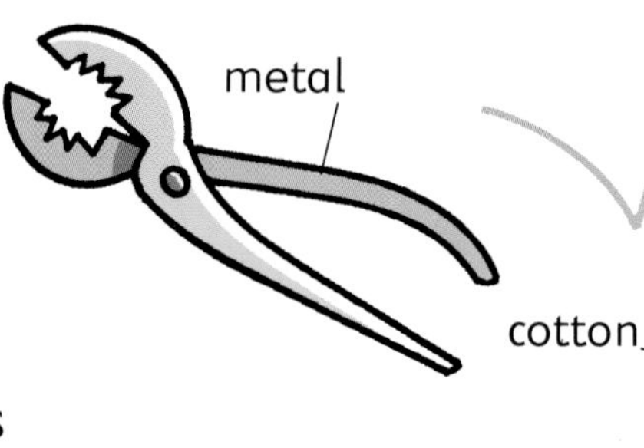

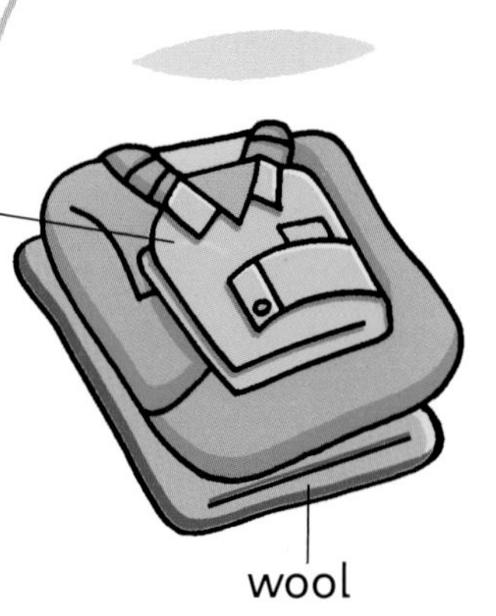

▲ Solids can be hard, like wood and metal, bouncy or stretchy like rubber, or soft, like wool and cotton.

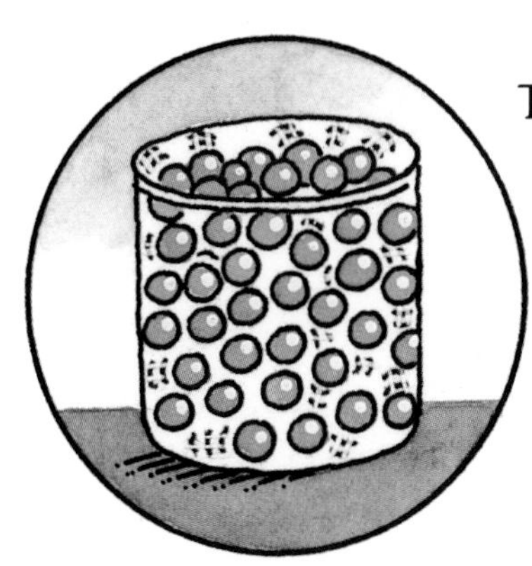

The atoms in liquids are not so closely linked. They move about more, so liquids flow. You need to put a liquid in a container to keep it from flowing away.

▲ There are many types of liquid. Some, like water, milk and petrol flow easily. Others, like syrup, are thick and sticky and flow slowly.

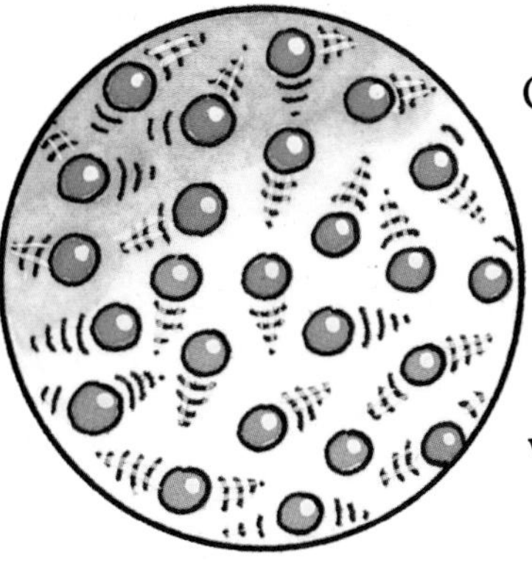

Gases are all around us, but they are not easy to see. The atoms in gases move around very quickly in all directions, so gases spread out to fill whatever space they are in.

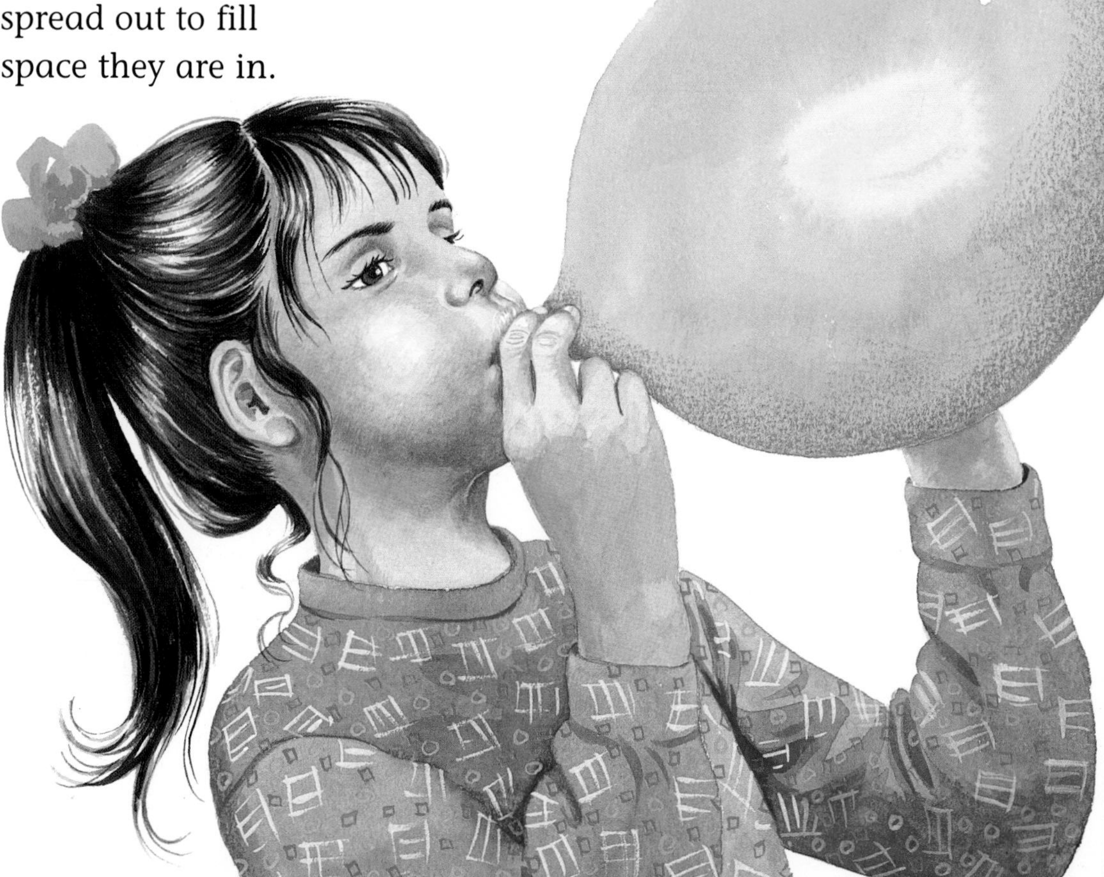

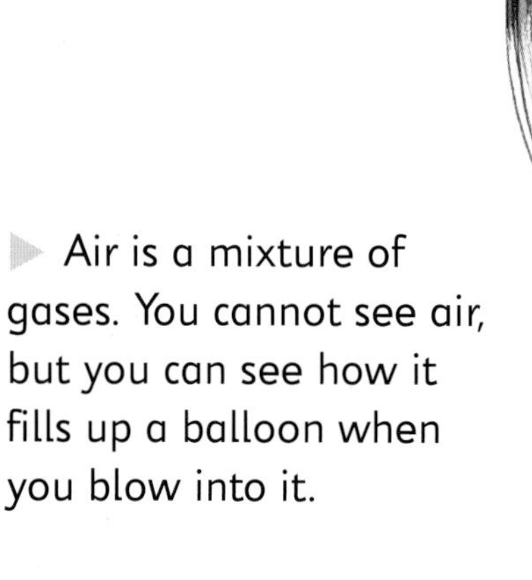

▶ Air is a mixture of gases. You cannot see air, but you can see how it fills up a balloon when you blow into it.

Water and air

Water is the most important liquid on Earth. We cannot live without it! Luckily, there is a lot of water on the Earth. Three-quarters of our planet is covered by oceans, seas, rivers and streams.

Air is the most important gas on Earth because all living things need it to breathe. There are several different gases in air. Nitrogen is the most common. But oxygen and carbon dioxide are the most important. Animals need to breathe oxygen to stay alive. Carbon dioxide helps plants to grow.

Clouds are made from tiny droplets of water, which rise up as water vapour from the oceans and seas. Eventually the water will fall to the ground again as rain.

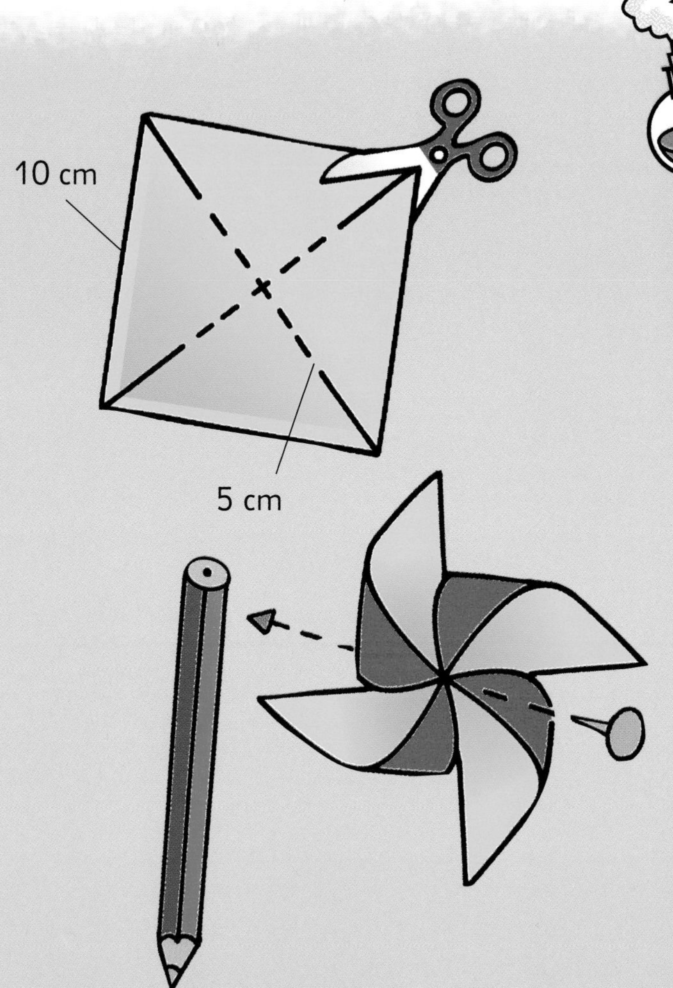

Try this: air power!

Wind is moving air. Make a pinwheel and see how air can make it turn.

1. Start with a square piece of paper with sides about 10 cm long.
Make diagonal cuts at each corner, as shown in the picture.
2. Fold every other corner into the centre of the square, then push a drawing pin through the centre and into the end of a pencil (it is easier if you use a pencil that has a rubber on the end).
3. If you blow on the pinwheel, the air in your breath will make it spin round. Take your pinwheel outside on a windy day – and see how the wind pushes the blades around.

Changing Materials

Heating and cooling materials can change them. Some materials change when they are put in water, too.

Melting and freezing

When you heat some solid materials they melt – when you cool them they become solid again. But the material is still the same, even after heating and cooling.

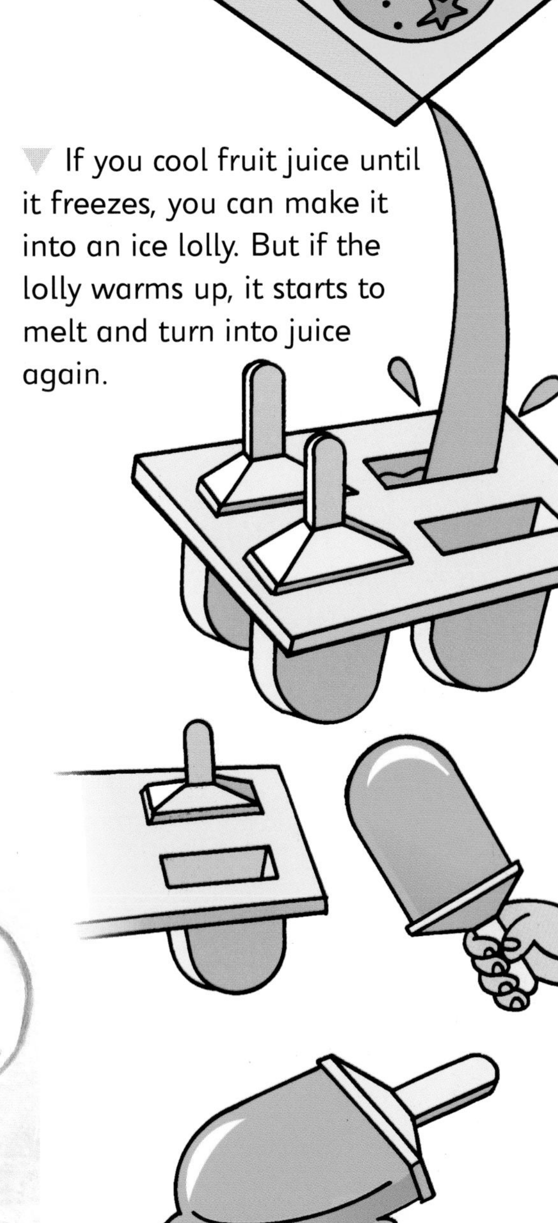

▼ If you cool fruit juice until it freezes, you can make it into an ice lolly. But if the lolly warms up, it starts to melt and turn into juice again.

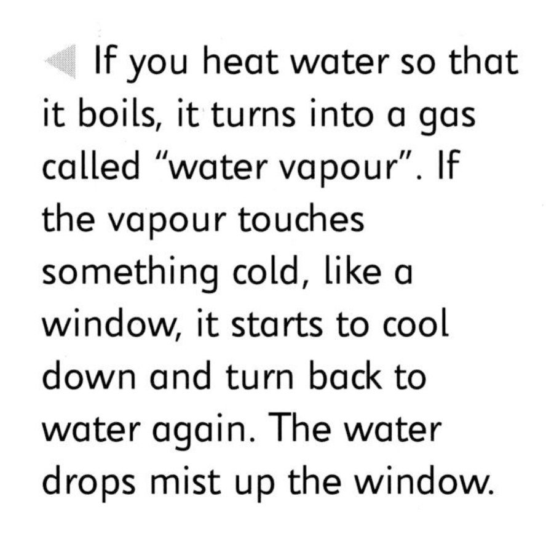

◄ If you heat water so that it boils, it turns into a gas called "water vapour". If the vapour touches something cold, like a window, it starts to cool down and turn back to water again. The water drops mist up the window.

Changed for ever

When some materials are heated, they are changed into different materials. If you heat a piece of paper so that it burns, it turns into ashes. The ashes cannot be changed back into paper even if you cool them.

Liquids can change when they are heated, too. When you crack an egg into a frying pan, it starts as a liquid, but the heat turns it into a solid. Even when you cool the egg down, it stays solid.

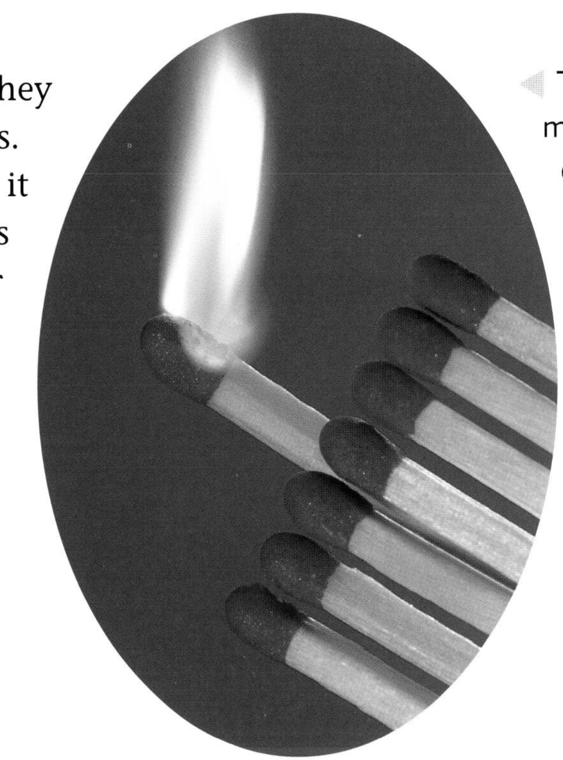

The head of a match contains chemicals that burn when you strike the match. These chemicals set the wood of the match burning.

Try this: disappearing salt

Some kinds of solid disappear when they are mixed with water. This is called " dissolving". But can you get the solid back again? Do this experiment and find out.

1. Pour a little warm water into a glass. Stir in a spoonful of salt until it disappears.

2. Dip your finger into the water to taste it. What does it taste like? What do you think happened to the salt?

3. Put a little salty water into a saucer and leave it a day or so until the water disappears. (The water has changed into water vapour and mixed with the air.) Taste a few of the white crystals left in the saucer. What do you think they are?

Making Materials

All the materials that people use come from raw materials. These are materials that we get out of the ground or take from plants and animals.

The cotton in your bath towel comes from a living plant. So does the wood for your bathroom shelf. The glass in your window is made from sand, soda and lime, which are dug out of the ground.

The pottery used to make plates and bowls is made out of clay. The plastics used to make your toothbrush came from a surprising raw material – oil! Oil is usually found deep under the ground.

Natural materials

Some raw materials can be made into useful things without changing them very much. We grow trees for their wood, and dig stone from the ground for building. We keep flocks of sheep for their wool. But before we can use these raw materials, they have to be collected, then cut and shaped in different ways.

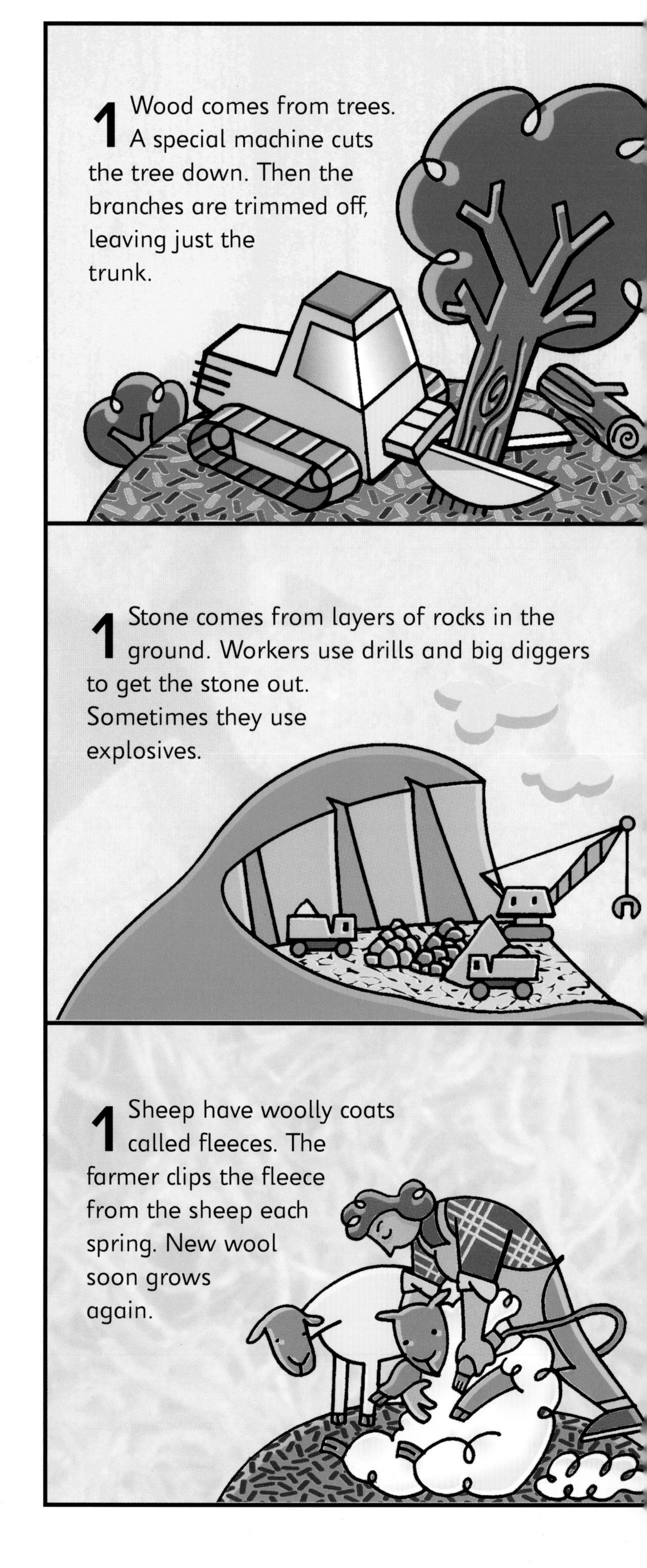

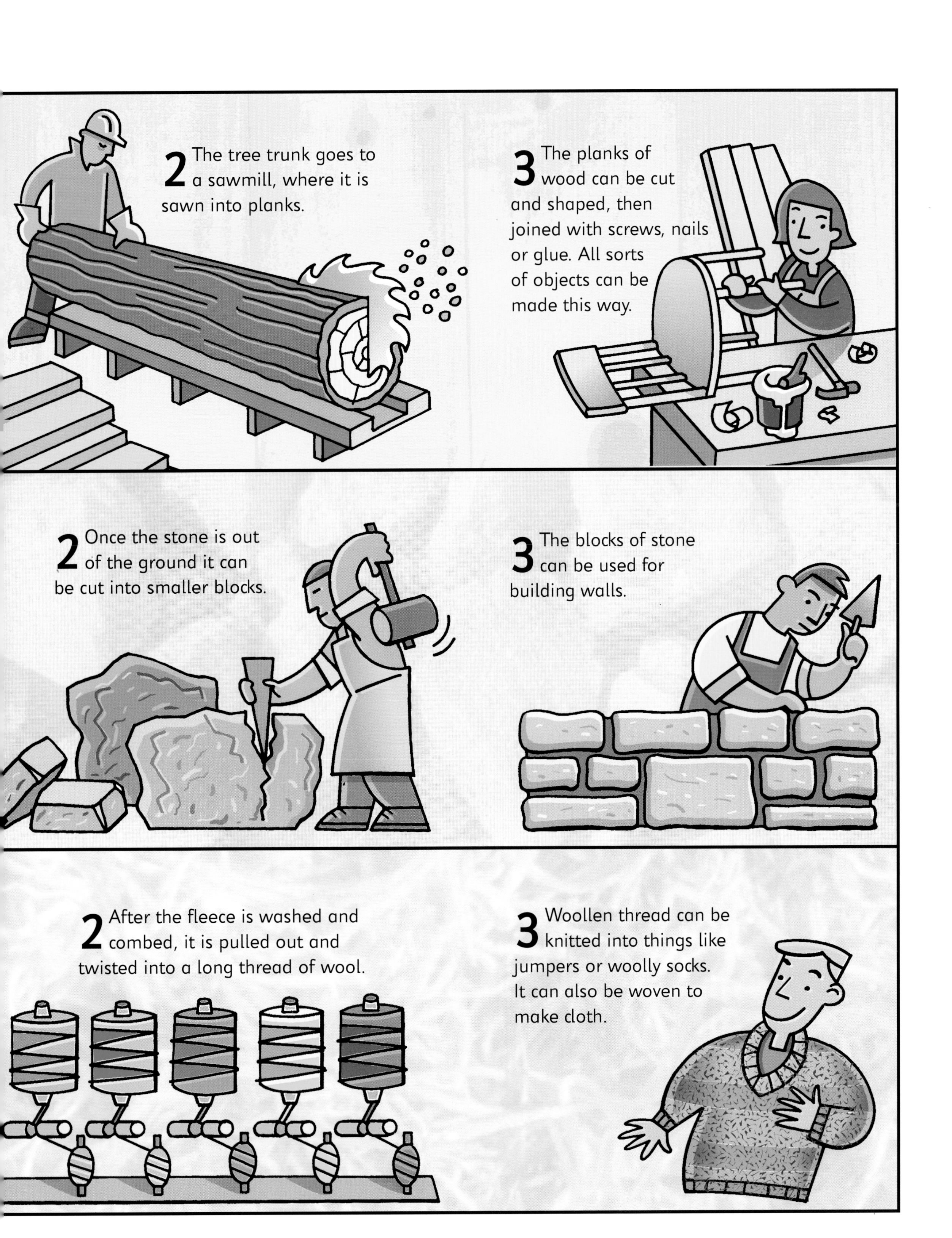
2 The tree trunk goes to a sawmill, where it is sawn into planks.
3 The planks of wood can be cut and shaped, then joined with screws, nails or glue. All sorts of objects can be made this way.
2 Once the stone is out of the ground it can be cut into smaller blocks.
3 The blocks of stone can be used for building walls.
2 After the fleece is washed and combed, it is pulled out and twisted into a long thread of wool.
3 Woollen thread can be knitted into things like jumpers or woolly socks. It can also be woven to make cloth.

New Materials

Some raw materials have to be changed a lot to make them into materials that are useful to us. This is done by mixing them with other materials, forming them into shapes and then heating them in different ways. The results can be surprising!

Minerals

Many of the raw materials we use come from substances called "minerals". These are natural substances found in rocks. Salt comes from rocks, and the graphite lead in your pencil. Most metals come from minerals, too.

Clay is a mineral. It is soft and wet, but if it is heated in a furnace it becomes harder and stronger.

Oil

Oil can be made into many different materials. First, the oil is heated to separate it into different chemicals. Then the different chemicals are made into paint, soap, glue, rubber and lots of other materials.

Plastics are materials made from oil. The plastic for these Lego pieces comes to the factory as tiny coloured beads. The beads are melted, then put into a mould of the right shape. The liquid sets hard into the new shape.

What's the difference?

These red bricks and this shiny basin are both made out of clay. But they look very different. Why?

These bricks are made by shaping soft, red clay into blocks. When they are dried and heated they turn into hard, strong blocks that can be used to build walls and houses.

This basin is also made of clay. After it has been made it is painted with a special mineral "paint", then heated again. The heat changes the mineral paint into a hard, shiny surface.

Metals

Metals are minerals too. They are found in rocks called "ores". The ores must be crushed or heated to collect the metal. Metals are often heated and mixed with other things to make new materials.

Steel is a very strong material. It is made by heating together iron ore, a rock called limestone and a kind of coal called coke in a huge furnace.

Pushes and Pulls

Get moving!

Cars drive by, dogs wag their tails, people stand up and walk around, someone rides past on a bicycle. Things are on the move all around us. You need pushes and pulls to get things moving. You also need pushes or pulls to make something that is already moving change direction, or slow down, or go faster.

Pushing and pulling are forces. When you kick a ball into the air, you give it a strong push. The push is a force. When you squeeze a lump of modelling clay you are using a force to make it change shape. When you pick up a pile of books, you can feel how much force you need to lift something.

Rubbing together

Friction is another kind of force. It happens when things rub against each other. Friction can slow things down and make them stop. Friction between your bike wheel and the brakes slows the bike down. But friction also helps the bike to grip the road, so that it can move along.

Gravity

There are other forces too. When you jump up into the air, a force called gravity pulls you back towards the ground again. When you kick a ball into the air, it comes down again because of gravity. Gravity pulls everything on the Earth towards the ground. No matter how high you kick a ball, gravity will always pull it back down.

If you let go of the branch, gravity pulls you to the ground.

Pulling can be very hard work!

Gravity does not pull astronauts in space down towards the ground. They float around as if they have no weight at all.

Simple Machines

Machines make work much easier. With a machine you can turn a small pull or push into a much bigger one. Machines can help you move something really heavy. They can also help you make things move faster. You can use very simple machines to help you do many kinds of things.

Give it a lift!

A lever is a simple machine that helps you lift heavy things. It is a long bar that rests on a turning point called a "pivot". To lift something heavy, you put one end under the thing you want to lift, and push down on the other end. The pivot needs to be close to the thing you are lifting.

▼ A seesaw is a kind of lever. You can use it to lift a heavy person up into the air. Try it!

Slippery slope

A slope is a simple machine that makes it easier to push heavy things upwards. Sliding things up a slope is a lot easier than lifting them!

Moving round

Wheels are simple machines. Wheels make it much easier to move heavy weights. You can join two wheels together using an axle, a rod that runs through the centre of each wheel.

▶ These removals men are using simple machines to help load heavy things into the van. The ramp into the van is a slope. And the trolley they are using has two wheels and an axle.

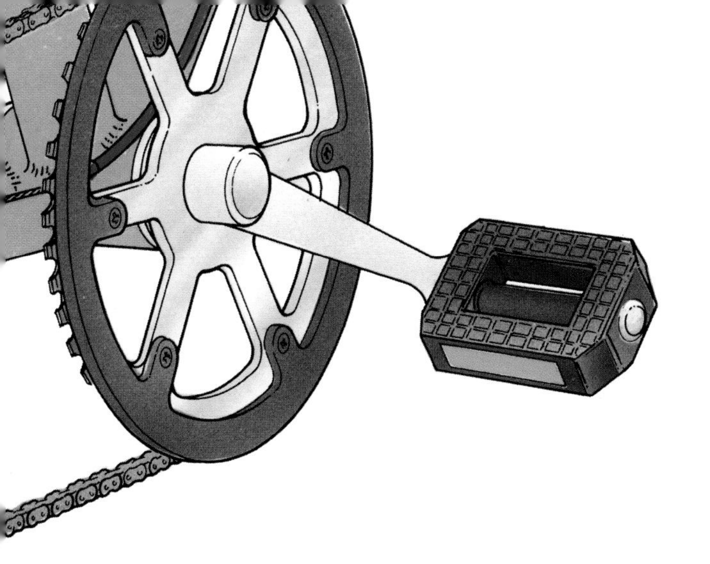

If you have gears on your bike, you do not need to pedal so fast when you whizz along on the flat. And gears make it much easier to ride your bike uphill.

Quick change

Gears are simple machines made out of toothed wheels. They are used to make one wheel turn faster or slower than another, or to make one wheel easier to turn than another. Gears are used in many machines – including bicycles.

Try this: a flying rubber!

You can use a ruler as a lever to throw things into the air.

You will need: *a ruler, a small box about 2 centimetres high, a rubber*

1. Set up your ruler as shown in the picture.

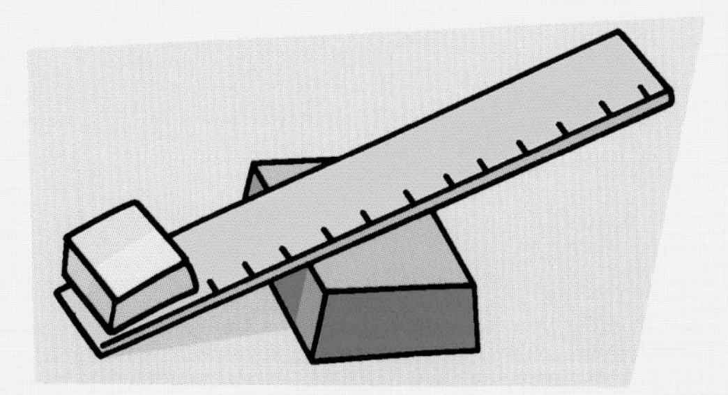

2. Give the upper end of the ruler a sharp tap. The rubber flies through the air!

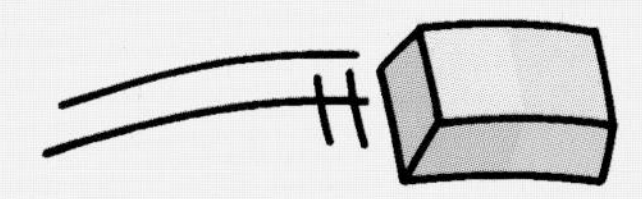

3. Try moving the lever so that the end on the table is closer to the pivot. Does the rubber fly higher or lower? What happens if you move the lever so that the end on the table is further away from the pivot?

Try using shooting something lighter than the rubber, like a button. Does it fly further, or not so far?

Pulling Power

Some machines help to move us around. These machines all need some kind of power to make them work. The power to make machines work can come from the wind, from water, from engines, from animals, or even from you!

There are all sorts of different ways to get about. Each one uses its own kind of pulling power.

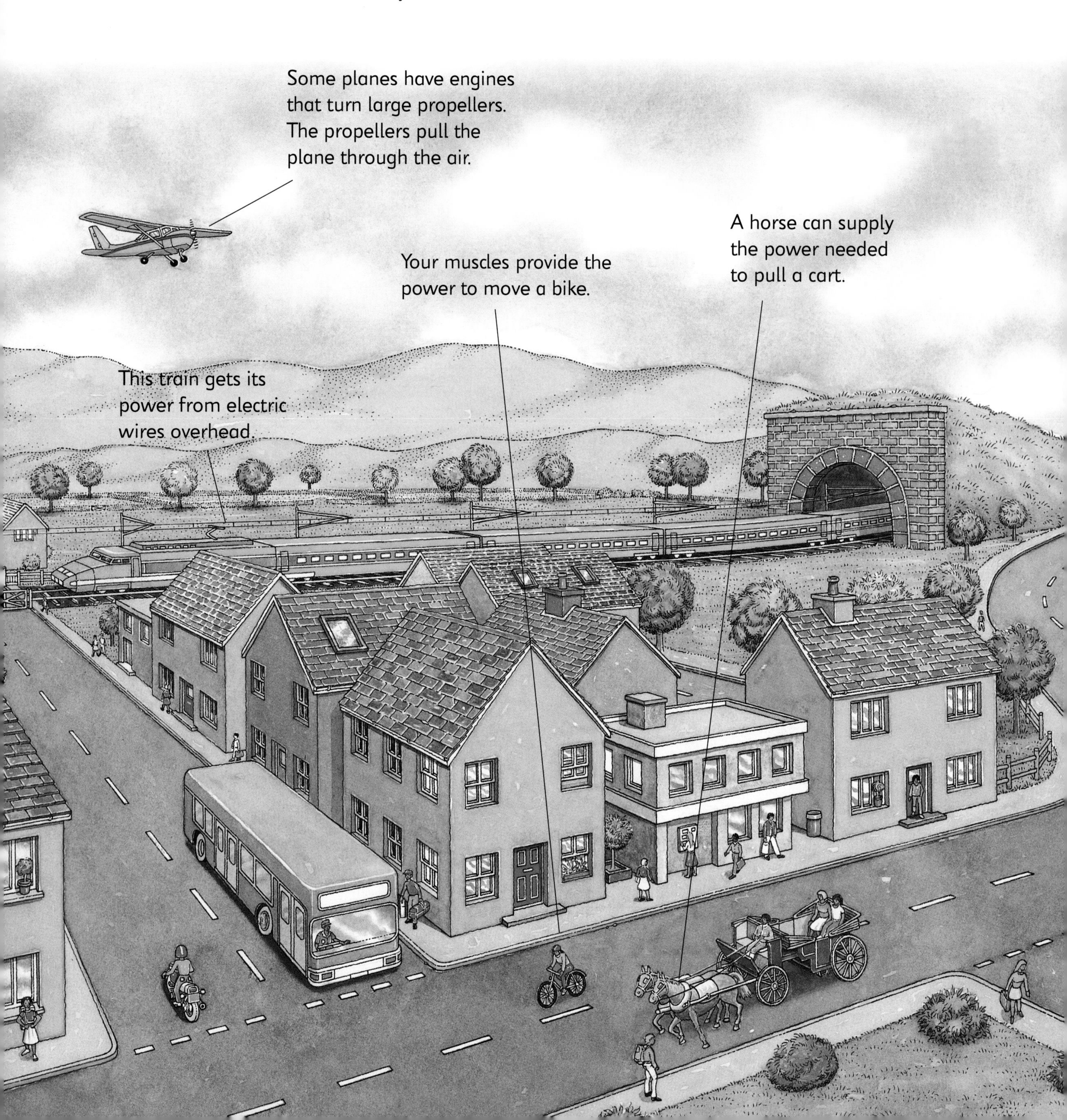

Engines

The power needed to run a machine can also come from an engine. Engines get their power from fuels. The engines that power cars, trucks and trains use petrol or diesel as their fuels. Some cars and trains use electricity to power their engines. Aircraft use a special kind of petrol for their engines.

Spacecraft blast into space using rockets – the most powerful engines of all.

Big airliners have jet engines. Air and hot gases shooting out of the back of the engine push the plane forwards.

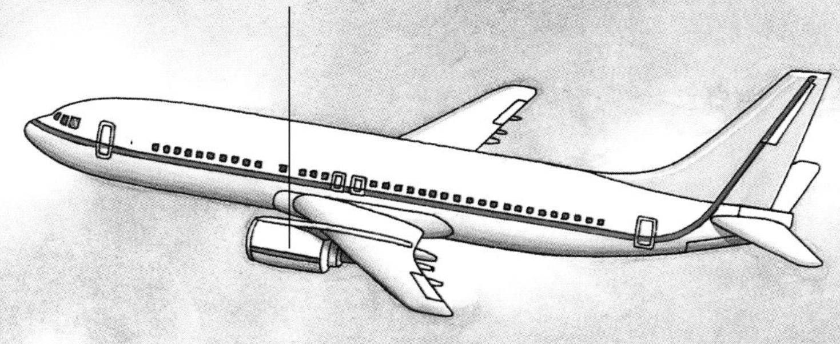

The engine in a boat turns a propeller. The propeller pushes the boat through the water.

The wind supplies the power needed to push a sailing boat through the water.

Try this: make a jet engine!

This simple jet engine is powered by air instead of hot gases.

You will need: *a balloon*

1. Blow up the balloon, then hold the end closed with your fingers. Do not tie it.

2. Let go of the balloon and watch it fly away. When you let go of the balloon the air inside rushes out and pushes the balloon along. The more air you blow into the balloon, the faster it will travel when you let it go.

Power Through a Wire

Every time you switch on a light, watch television or listen to a CD, you are using electricity. Electricity is a very handy form of energy, because it can travel through wires to where it is needed. And when you don't need electricity – you can switch it off!

Mains or battery?

Most of the electricity used in your house travels through wires hidden in the walls to power points or sockets. This is called "mains electricity". You can also get electricity from batteries. Batteries use chemicals to make electricity. When you use batteries, you don't have to plug anything into a socket on the wall. This makes them good for things that you carry around.

Most of the machines in your house – washing machines, refrigerators, toasters and televisions – run on electricity. So do many other machines outside.

With batteries in your cassette player, you can have music wherever you go.

Play safe!

Mains electricity can be very dangerous. Never touch bare wires or electric sockets or plugs. You may get an electric shock. Always ask a grown-up to help you when you use electricity.

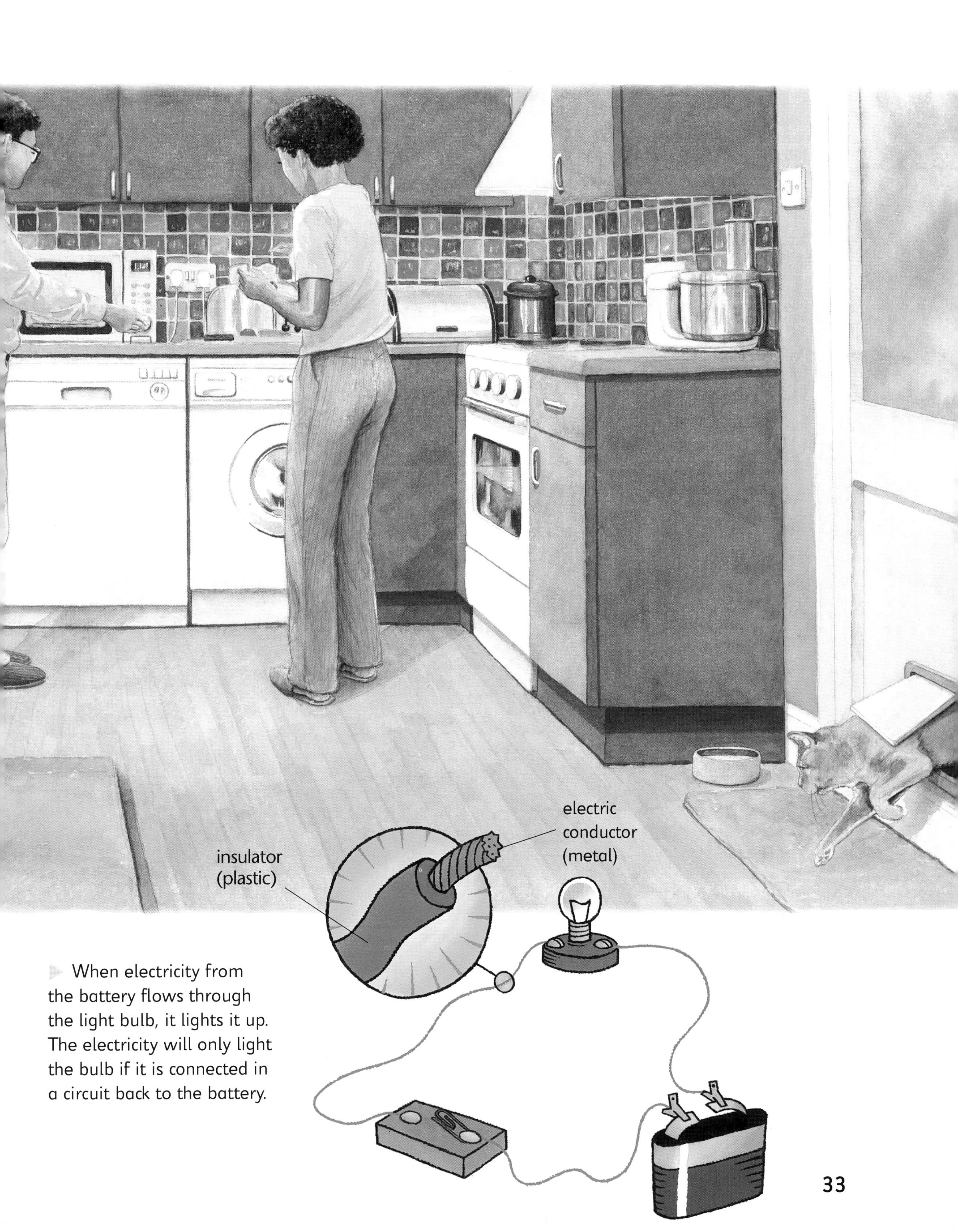

When electricity from the battery flows through the light bulb, it lights it up. The electricity will only light the bulb if it is connected in a circuit back to the battery.

Where Does Electricity Come From?

The electricity made in power stations travels to houses, shops and factories along metal wires called "power lines". Tall pylons hold the power lines up. Machines called "transformers" change the strength of the electricity travelling along the wires.

The electricity we use in our houses comes from special factories called power stations. It is made by a machine called a generator. Another machine, called a turbine, turns the generator to produce electricity.

Turning the turbines

Different power stations use different kinds of power to make the turbine spin. Most power stations burn fuels like coal or oil to heat water and make steam. A jet of steam then pushes the turbine round.

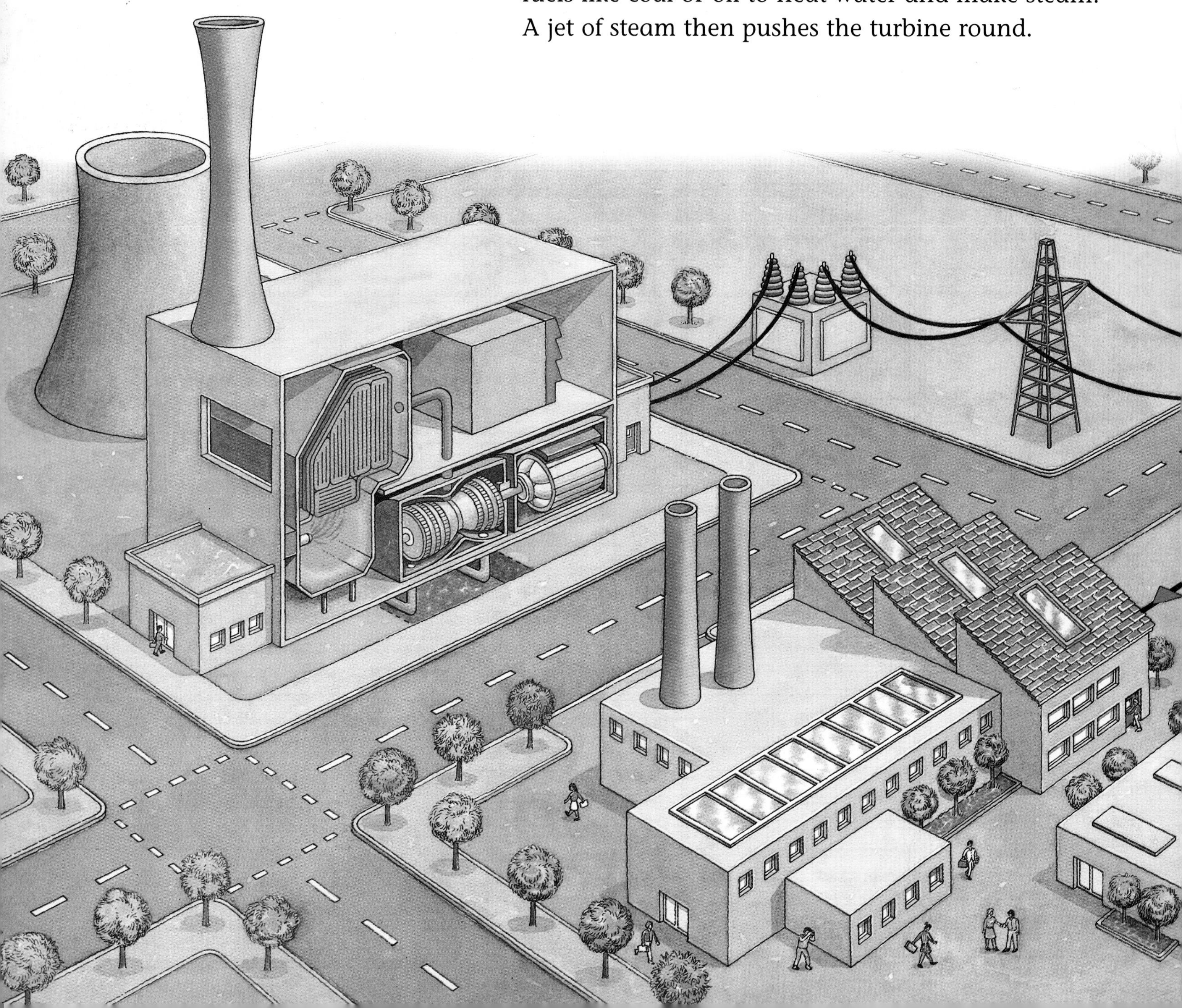

Power from water, the wind and the Sun

In some places electricity is made using energy from the wind or water. In hydroelectric power stations, for instance, rushing water turns the turbines. Light from the Sun or heat from below the Earth's surface can be used to make electricity, too. Making electricity using these kinds of power causes less pollution than burning fuels. But they cannot produce all the electricity we need.

These special windmills are turned by the power of the wind. Each windmill turns a generator to make electricity.

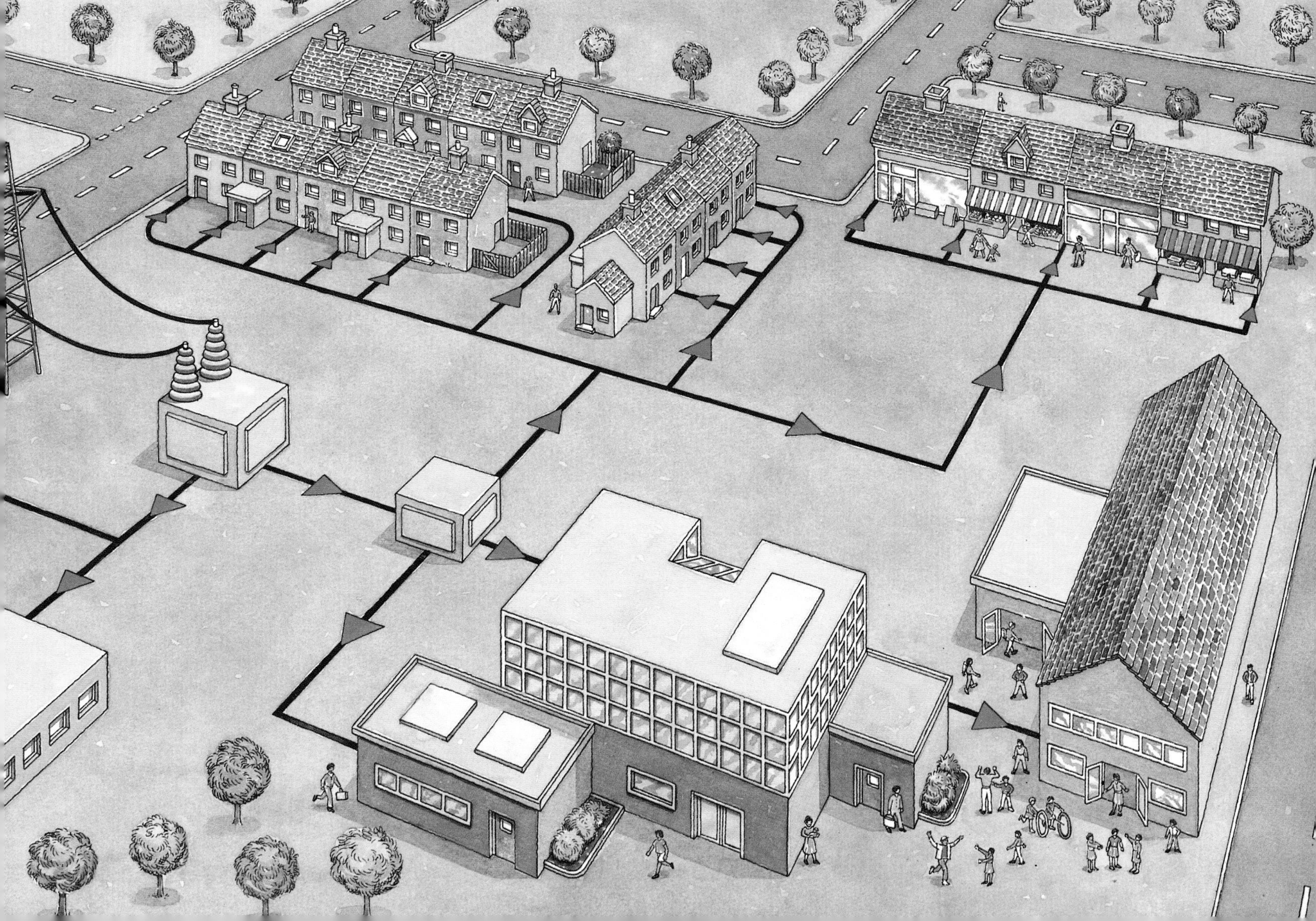

Light

Light is a type of energy that lets us see. Lots of the light on Earth comes from the Sun. When we cannot see the Sun, we have to find other ways to get light. The Sun gives us a very bright light because it is very, very hot. Luckily, other things can get hot and give off light too.

In a light bulb, electricity flows through a coil of thin wire. The wire gets hot and gives off light. The candle flame in the lantern gets very hot, and so is the fire in the fireplace. Both of them give off light.

Speedy light

Light travels very fast. Even though the Sun is millions of kilometres away, it takes less than 9 minutes for sunlight to reach us on Earth. Flashes of light sent from tens of kilometres away reach your eyes almost as soon as they are sent.

Bouncy light

You can only see something if light bounces off it and into your eyes. When the light goes into your eyes, it sends signals to your brain. The signals make it possible for you to see things. Without light you could not see anything at all.

Colour-full light

Sunlight looks white, but is really a mixture of colours. When sunlight shines through drops of water, it splits up and you can see all the different colours of the rainbow.

During the day, light from the Sun lights up the world.

Try this:

Make your own rainbow

Try this experiment on a sunny day.

You will need: *a shallow dish of water, a small mirror, a piece of paper.*

1. Put the dish of water next to a window and put the small mirror into it so that the mirror faces the Sun. Do <u>not</u> look into the mirror.

2. Hold the piece of paper above the dish and move the mirror so that the light reflected off the mirror shines onto the paper. What colours do you see on the paper? Does it look like a rainbow in the sky?

Shadows and Reflections

When you walk on a sunny day with the Sun behind you, you can see your shadow in front of you. Where did it come from? Your shadow appears because your body blocks the light.

Sunlight cannot shine through you. Light only travels in straight lines, so it cannot bend around you. Trees, cars, buildings and bikes all have shadows too. In fact, anything that light cannot shine through will have a shadow.

Light does shine through some things – like clear glass. But light only partly shines through other things – like paper.

Night and day

The Sun can only light up one side of the Earth at a time. On the side where the Sun shines, it is day. On the side that is in shadow, it is night. But the Earth is not still – it spins around once every 24 hours. So everywhere on Earth is lit for part of this 24-hour day. When the place you live faces the Sun, it is daytime. When it faces away from the Sun, it is night.

Imagine you have a cousin living on the other side of the Earth. When you go to school, your cousin will be fast asleep in bed. This is because when it is night on one side of the Earth, it is daytime on the other.

Reflections

When you stand in front of a mirror, light from your body bounces off the mirror and into your eyes, so you can see your reflection. Other shiny surfaces reflect light too. Where else can you see your reflection?

On dark nights the Moon may be very bright, but it is not really giving off light. It just looks bright because light from the Sun is reflected off it.

Try this: shadow puppets

It is easy to make shadow puppets that look like funny animals. You can even add voices, and hold a puppet show for your friends.

You will need: *a flat, light-coloured wall, a torch, your hands.*

1. Shine the light on the wall.

2. Put your hand in front of the light and move it forwards until your hand makes a clear and sharp shadow.

3. Move your fingers into different shapes to look like animals.

Sound

Listen carefully. Do you hear birds singing? Can you hear someone talking, or music playing? Can you hear the whoosh as the wind blows? Sounds can be loud or soft, gentle or unpleasant. But they are all made by something vibrating, or moving quickly to and fro.

Shaking sounds

Something has to vibrate to make a sound. If you stretch a rubber band between your fingers and pluck it, you can see it vibrate as it hums. If you put your fingers on your throat as you talk or sing, you can feel the vibrations.

When something vibrates, it makes waves in the air. These sound waves travel through the air to your ears, and you hear a sound!

◀ You can make sound vibrations by shaking things, or by banging things together. Or you can hit something hollow, such as a drum or a bell.

Slow sounds

Sounds do not travel as quickly as light. Sometimes you have to wait to hear them. During a thunderstorm, you may see flashes of lightning before you hear thunder. You see flashes of lightning right away, because light travels so fast. The thunder takes longer to reach you because sound travels more slowly.

Next time there is a thunderstorm nearby, count the seconds between seeing the lightning flash and hearing the thunder. For every 3 seconds you count, the storm is 1 kilometre away.

Try it out: play a tune

How many different sounds can you make with this rubber band banjo?

You will need: *an empty margarine tub without a lid, some thick and some thin rubber bands, and plasticine.*

Put a thick rubber band around the margarine tub. Pluck the rubber band and listen to the sound. If you pull on the rubber band to make it tighter, what happens to the sound? (You can use lumps of plasticine to help hold the rubber band tight). Can you pull on the rubber band by different amounts to play a tune?

Try using a thin rubber band instead of a thick one. Does the note sound higher or lower? Then try putting several different rubber bands around the tub. Can you find a way to play a tune on them?

Invisible messengers

It would be difficult to shout a message to someone standing several kilometres away because the sound waves wouldn't travel far enough. But there are other kinds of wave, such as radio waves and microwaves, that can travel much further. These invisible messengers help us to speak and listen to each other all over the world. They let us talk on mobile phones, and even help us send and receive messages from space!

Tuning in

Radio waves are not just used for radios. They also carry sounds and pictures to your television from a television station many kilometres away. The picture below shows how this happens.

▼ At the television station, a TV camera changes the pictures it sees into electrical signals. These go to a transmitting aerial on top of a tall mast. The aerial sends the signals out in all directions as radio waves. An aerial on your house picks up the signals and your television changes them back into pictures.

Many different programmes are broadcast at the same time. You choose what programme you want to listen to by tuning your radio or changing the channels on your television.

Microwaves

We use microwaves for cooking, in microwave ovens. But microwaves can be used in other ways, too. Mobile phones send messages using microwaves. Radar uses microwaves to detect aircraft and ships even when it is dark or foggy.

Microwave oven.

Mobile phone.

Radar aerial.

Radio waves can carry television and radio programmes around the world by bouncing them off satellites in space, so they travel back to Earth again.

Important Words

aerial: something that is used to send or receive radio and other kinds of wave that carry messages.

air: a mixture of gases made up mainly of nitrogen and oxygen with small amounts of other gases such as carbon dioxide.

astronomer: a scientist who studies the stars and planets.

atoms: the tiniest possible piece of a thing.

battery: a device that uses chemicals to make and store electricity. Batteries are useful for providing power for machines that you carry around.

biologist: a scientist who studies living things.

cells: tiny parts that make up all living things.

chemist: a scientist who studies what things are made of.

conductor: a material that electricity can travel through easily.

dissolve: to mix something into a liquid so that it becomes part of the liquid and seems to disappear.

droplets: tiny drops of a liquid.

electricity: a handy form of energy that travels through wires. Electricity can be used to produce heat and light and to run many different kinds of machine.

energy: the strength to do things, or the power to do work.

engine: something that provides the power needed to run a machine. A motor is a kind of engine.

explosives: things that can be made to let off lots of energy in a sudden burst.

fleece: the woolly coat of a sheep.

force: the power or strength that makes something move, change direction, slow down or go faster.

fuel: something that gives power to an engine. Petrol and diesel are fuels. So are coal, wood and electricity.

freeze: to cool a liquid until it becomes a solid.

gases: substances that spread to fill whatever space they are in. The atoms in gases move around very quickly in all directions.

generator: a machine that produces electricity.

geologist: a scientist who studies the Earth. Geologists look at rocks. They also study volcanoes and earthquakes.

insulator: a material that electricity cannot travel through.

light: a type of energy that travels very fast and lets us see.

liquids: substances that flow away unless they are in a container. The atoms in liquids are not so closely linked as they are in solids.

machine: something that can be used to help move things more easily or to make work easier.

materials: substances There are many different types of materials.

mathematician: a scientist who studies numbers, shapes and the patterns they make.

melt: to heat a solid material so that it turns into a liquid.

minerals: natural materials found in rocks. Metals are a kind of mineral. Salt and diamonds are minerals, too.

mixture: several different things mixed together. Each of the things in the mixture is not changed, so it can be separated out again.

ores: rocks that have useful minerals, such as metals, in them.

physicist: a scientist who studies movement and energy and heat and sound.

pivot: a turning point.

planks: flat pieces, or boards, of wood.

pollution: chemicals or tiny pieces of substances that make something dirty. Pollution is caused in many different ways. Oil spilled from ships causes pollution. So does the exhaust from cars.

power: the energy or strength needed to make a machine work or to move something.

propellers: turning blades that pull a plane through the air or push a boat through the water.

raw materials: materials we get out of the ground or take from plants or animals that are used to make other things.

reflection: something you see when light bounces off a shiny surface.

reproduce: to have babies.

satellites: objects that travel, or orbit, around the Earth in space. Satellites are used to study things on Earth and to help send radio and television signals around the world.

science: the study of things and happenings that can be looked at and tested.

scientist: someone who uses science to find out things.

shadow: the dark area that appears when something blocks light.

solids: substances that can keep their shape outside of a container. The atoms in solids are closely linked together.

sounds: noise. Sounds are produced when something vibrates.

transformer: a machine that changes the 'strength' of electricity travelling along a wire.

transmitting aerial: an aerial used to send out signals.

vapour: a kind of gas, like steam or mist, that you can see.

vibrate: to move quickly backwards and forwards or side to side.

womb: the part of a mother's body where babies grow.

Index

Acknowledgements

Photos
Pages 19tr Michael Marten/SPL; 21tr Tek Image/SPL; 24bl Klaus Guldbrandsen/SPL; 25br Rosenfeld Images Ltd/SPL; 27br NASA; 31tr NASA; 35br Russell D Curtis/SPL; 39tr NASA; 40–41tc Keith Kent/SPL; 43br SPL.

Artwork
Pages 6 and 7tl Patricia Ludlow; 7b John Haslam; 8 Tony Kerrins; 9l Tony Kerrins; 9r John Haslam; 10 John Haslam; 11t Patricia Ludlow; 11t overlay Steve Weston; 11b Chris Forsey; 12t Lynne Willey; 12tr overlay Steve Weston; 12b Steve Weston; 13t John Haslam; 13b Tony Kerrins; 13b overlay Steve Weston; 14t Steve Weston; 14–15 Tony Kerrins; 15cr Lynne Willey; 16b John Haslam; 16–17 Patricia Ludlow; 17b John Haslam; 18t John Haslam; 18tr John Haslam; 18b Lynne Willey; 19b John Haslam; 20tr John Haslam; 20 l Jenny Gregory; 21b John Haslam; 22–23 John Haslam; 24t Jane Cope; 25t Jane Cope; 26–27 Jane Cope; 28bl Lynne Willey; 28–29t Nick Hawken; 28–29b Lynne Willey; 29r John Haslam; 30–31 Jason Lewis; 32–33 Jenny Gregory; 33b Clive Goodyer; 34–35 Jason Lewis; 36tl John Walker; 36bl Jenny Gregory; 37t James Sneddon; 37l John Haslam; 37r Jenny Gregory; 38t Tony Kerrins; 38b Julian Baum; 39b Lynne Willey; 40b Annabel Spenceley; 41r John Haslam; 42 Jason Lewis; 43t John Haslam.